DOGS SET IX

IRISH RED AND WHITE SETTERS

Joanne Mattern
ABDO Publishing Company

Printed in the United States of America, North Mankato, Minnesota.
062011
092011

 PRINTED ON RECYCLED PAPER

Cover Photo: NyaStar IRWS: Kellyn Miller & Shawn Hazen
Interior Photos: Alamy p. 5; NyaStar IRWS: Kellyn Miller & Shawn Hazen pp. 9, 11, 13, 15, 17, 19, 20, 21; Thinkstock p. 7

Editors: Megan M. Gunderson, BreAnn Rumsch
Art Direction: Neil Klinepier

Library of Congress Cataloging-in-Publication Data

Mattern, Joanne, 1963-
  Irish red and white setters / Joanne Mattern.
     p. cm. -- (Dogs)
  Includes index.
  ISBN 978-1-61714-991-7
  1. Irish setters--Juvenile literature. I. Title.
SF429.I7.M38 2012
636.752'6--dc22
                                        2011010097

CONTENTS

THE DOG FAMILY

Today, more than 400 different dog **breeds** live around the world. They range in size from extra small to extra large.

Incredibly, all of these dogs are part of the family **Canidae**. This name comes from the Latin word *canis*, which means "dog." Coyotes, foxes, and wolves are also part of this family. In fact, scientists believe all dogs descended from the gray wolf.

Dogs are extremely popular pets. In the United States alone, people own about 75 million dogs! Humans and dogs have been companions for more than 12,000 years. During that time, dogs have served as protectors, herders, fishers, and hunters.

The Irish red and white setter is a hunting **breed**. A setter locates a bird and then sets, or lays down, and looks at it. This helps the hunter locate the **game**. The Irish red and white setter is also a popular family pet with a proud, rich history.

Irish red and white setters are known as gun dogs or pointing dogs.

Irish Red and White Setters

Long ago in Ireland, hunters depended on dogs to help them hunt. By the late 1600s, setters were a popular choice.

Some setters were all red. Others were red and white. Eventually, these different-colored dogs became known as two separate **breeds**. They are the Irish setter and the Irish red and white setter.

Hunters preferred the red and white dogs. But by the mid-1800s, the red Irish setter was more popular with breeders. So, the Irish red and white setter almost became extinct.

Then during the 1920s, people worked hard to bring back this breed. About twenty years later, the Irish red and white setter once again became

6

Irish red and white setters are closely related to Irish setters (right). Both descended from a type of dog called a spaniel.

popular. In fact, the Irish Red and White Setter Society officially formed in 1944.

Today, the **breed** is well established around the world. In 2009, the **American Kennel Club (AKC)** recognized the Irish red and white setter. The AKC assigned this gun dog to its sporting group.

What They're Like

Irish red and white setters need a lot of attention. They are friendly dogs that usually get along well with people. They enjoy being around their families, and they make sweet, loving, loyal pets.

These lively, energetic dogs are also good with children. So, Irish red and white setters are great pets for families with active kids. They love to play fetch and learn other games.

This spirited **breed** is also very smart! It is important to train the Irish red and white setter to follow commands. It will learn best from an owner who is calm but firm.

Lots of exercise is key for this active, playful breed!

COAT AND COLOR

An Irish red and white setter has a **parti-color** coat. The coat is white with chestnut-red patches called islands. The head and ears are usually red. The tail may be all white, but a red patch is preferred.

Sometimes tiny flecks, or spots, of red fur are found around the face. The feet and legs can also have flecks up to the elbow or the **hock**.

Most of this **breed**'s coat is short and either flat or wavy. The long, silky fur on the back of the legs is called feathering. There is feathering on the tail and the outer side of the ears, too.

Longer fur can easily become tangled or **matted**. So, owners may need to groom their Irish red and white setters daily.

Feathering on the dog's chest and throat is known as a fringe.

SIZE

Irish red and white setters are large dogs. They usually weigh between 60 and 70 pounds (27 and 32 kg). Male Irish red and white setters are about 24 to 26 inches (61 to 66 cm) tall at the shoulders. Females stand about 22 to 24 inches (56 to 61 cm) tall.

This **breed** is known for being athletic and powerful. Long legs support this dog's deep chest and long, muscular neck and body. The medium-length tail tapers to a point. It is carried level with the dog's back.

This dog also has a broad head and a long, square **muzzle**. Its nose is black or dark brown. Its ears drop to a medium length. They are set level with the dog's round, dark hazel or dark brown eyes.

The Irish red and white setter is prized as a skilled, enthusiastic hunter.

CARE

Irish red and white setters are generally healthy dogs. Sometimes they have vision problems such as cataracts. And puppies can inherit **von Willebrand disease** from their parents.

The best way to maintain your dog's good health is to see a veterinarian at least once a year. The veterinarian will give the dog **vaccines**. He or she will also **spay** or **neuter** dogs that are not going to be **bred**.

Regular grooming is another important part of your Irish red and white setter's care. Give your dog a bath every few weeks or when its coat gets dirty. Brush your pet's teeth to keep them healthy. Also, keep your dog's nails short and ears clean.

Finally, make daily exercise a priority. These tireless dogs like to take long, brisk walks. It is a good idea to let this **breed** run and play in a fenced area, too.

Irish red and white setters love physical activity and time near people.

FEEDING

Active Irish red and white setters need high-quality food to stay healthy and strong. Dry, canned, or semimoist foods are all good options for this **breed**.

Puppies usually eat three or four times a day until they are six months old. Then, they eat two meals daily until they reach adulthood. Most adult dogs eat one main meal a day. But, it is okay to split a large dog's food into two smaller meals.

Water is important for all dogs. Irish red and white setters should always have a bowl of clean, fresh water to drink. This is especially important during hot weather or after your dog has exercised.

*Fresh food and water support your puppy as it grows
into a healthy adult Irish red and white setter.*

THINGS THEY NEED

Obedience training is important for all dogs. For Irish red and white setters, good training is essential. An untrained Irish red and white setter may become bored or destructive.

These dogs are happier and easier to live with if they know the rules and know who's the boss. Training may require more time with this mild-mannered **breed** than other gun dogs. The Irish red and white setter needs patient, gentle handling.

Before getting an Irish red and white setter, you should buy a leash and a collar. You will also need a license for your dog. Provide a comfortable bed, bowls for food and water, and plenty of toys. Your new dog will feel right at home!

**Basic commands your dog
should learn include
"sit," "stay," and "heel."**

PUPPIES

New puppies are dependent on their mother.

Irish red and white setters are **pregnant** for about 63 days. A female usually gives birth to six to ten puppies.

Like other **breeds**, Irish red and white setter puppies cannot see or hear for two to three weeks. They have to stay with their mother until they are six to eight weeks old. By then, the puppies can hear, see, and run around. They are also eating solid food instead of nursing.

Happy Irish red and white setters have a lot of love to give to the right owner!

Owners should **socialize** their Irish red and white setter puppies. It is important to introduce them to other people and animals. Trips to different places are a good idea, too. This helps the puppies learn about the world around them. A healthy, well-trained Irish red and white setter will be a loving companion for 12 to 13 years.

GLOSSARY

American Kennel Club (AKC) - an organization that studies and promotes interest in purebred dogs.

breed - a group of animals sharing the same ancestors and appearance. A breeder is a person who raises animals. Raising animals is often called breeding them.

Canidae (KAN-uh-dee) - the scientific Latin name for the dog family. Members of this family are called canids. They include wolves, jackals, foxes, coyotes, and domestic dogs.

game - wild animals hunted for food or sport.

hock - a joint in a hind leg of a four-legged animal. A hock is similar to a knee joint, except that it bends backward.

matted - forming a tangled mass.

muzzle - an animal's nose and jaws.

neuter (NOO-tuhr) - to remove a male animal's reproductive glands.

parti-color - having a dominant color broken up by patches of one or more other colors.

pregnant - having one or more babies growing within the body.

socialize - to accustom an animal or a person to spending time with others.

spay - to remove a female animal's reproductive organs.

vaccine (vak-SEEN) - a shot given to prevent illness or disease.

von Willebrand disease - a condition marked by blood clotting problems and excessive bruising.

WEB SITES

To learn more about Irish red and white setters, visit ABDO Publishing Company online. Web sites about Irish red and white setters are featured on our Book Links page. These links are routinely monitored and updated to provide the most current information available.

www.abdopublishing.com

INDEX